When Being A Grandma
Isn't So Grand
4 Keys to L.O.V.E. Your
Grandchild's Parents

When Being A Grandma Isn't So Grand 4 Keys to L.O.V.E. Your Grandchild's Parents

by

Donne Davis

ISBN 978-1-300069-294

Cover art © 2012 Ron Leishman of ToonClipart.com

Dedication

To my daughter and son-in-law, Deborah and Matt, who invited me to join them on the most fascinating journey of my life, becoming "Baba," and to my two precious granddaughters, Juliet and Amelia, who've brought me more joy and laughter than I ever could have wished for.

Contents

Acknowledgements

I have wanted to write a book for as long as I can remember. But it wasn't until I met Alison Marks that I finally began to formulate a plan and learn about the tools and resources I needed to make it happen. At Alison's workshop, I sat next to Amira Alvarez who inspired me with her excellent coaching. Alison introduced me to Candace Davenport who encouraged me to keep working and dream bigger. Candace helped me find my excellent copyeditor, Linda Jay Geldens.

It was pure serendipity that led me to Ron Leishman, (ToonClipart.com) the artist who designed the whimsical cover for this book.

I'm grateful to all of the grandmas I've met over the past nine years—especially the members of the GaGa Sisterhood who've shared their joys and challenges with me so openly and willingly. They continue to inspire me with their wisdom.

I'm also grateful to all the moms who took the time to respond so honestly to my survey. Their insight gave me a new perspective on the grandparent relationship.

I feel such gratitude for my dearest friend Marilyn, who has always believed in me and encouraged me by saying "I know you're going to write that book someday!"

But most of all, I want to acknowledge the people in my family who made this book possible: my two beloved grandmothers,

Amelia and Gertrude, who I was blessed to have in my life until I was forty; my mother, Julie, who continues to inspire me with her inner strength and resilience; my daughter, Deborah, who has been one of my wisest teachers over the past decade; and most of all, my dear husband, Sonny, who has been my number one cheerleader since the day we met over four decades ago. I am so blessed to have him as my coach, sounding board, editor, designer and tech wizard.

My purpose in writing this book is to share both sides of the grandparent relationship, so that grandmas can understand how moms feel and in turn, moms can understand how grandmas feel. I figure that when we understand each other's perspectives, we can then focus on our shared purpose: *nurturing our grandchildren, those precious human beings who share our DNA.*

Also, throughout this book there are endnotes to links with relevant resources that can help both grandmas and moms grow comfortably into their new roles.

Preface

In 2003 I began an amazing journey. I became a grandma. I had just retired from my job as a college recruiter and was looking forward to joining my husband in his blissful state of retirement. We wanted to travel and explore the world together.

When I wished for travel, I guess I should have been more specific about where I wanted to go. Actually, I *have* traveled since I retired, but mostly back and forth on Interstate 80 to visit my two granddaughters! Even though I was not heading to exotic destinations, those trips on I-80 were certainly filled with adventure. I've written stories about every one of those visits in spiral journals[1] that I plan to give to the girls when they're older. And during every visit, I learned a new lesson about my role as a grandma.

Becoming a modern grandma has been a fascinating growth experience that involves not only getting to know and love my precious grandchildren, but also learning to love and understand my daughter and son-in-law as they evolve into their new roles.

Remember that parents these days have access to a wealth of information that can sometimes sound like a foreign language to new grandparents. So many changes have occurred since we raised our own children. It can take a while to get up to speed and understand what's going on without having to ask, or challenge, the new parents about what they're doing in terms of discipline and goals.

I've made many mistakes along the way—offering advice when it wasn't requested, buying the wrong kinds of gifts, and questioning my children's parenting methods. I've readily admitted my mistakes (believe me, that gets easier with practice) and I've asked my daughter for forgiveness numerous times. This is all a humbling experience and provides a good role model for your children and grandchildren.

As a new grandma, I had no idea how complicated my role would be. I observed my own two grandmas for nearly four decades, but they made grandparenting seem like a piece of cake—a treat I got offered a lot, by the way, whenever I visited my grandparents' homes. Nowadays, if you want to serve your grandchildren cake, you'd better clear it with their parents first!

The moment I became a grandma, I embraced my role with energy and enthusiasm. First, I read all the books I could find about grandparenting. At the same time, I wondered what other grandmas were experiencing. Since I had come of age in the era of consciousness-raising groups, I wanted reassurance that all the emotions I was feeling were "normal."

As I saw the proliferation of mothers' clubs over the past two decades, I recognized that they provided three important solutions to pressing needs: an escape from isolation, an empathetic ear, and resources to help cope with all of the challenges mothers face.

Grandmas have needs, too. We want to make friends with other grandmas so we can *kvell* and *kvetch* about our joys and challenges. *Kvell* and *kvetch* are Yiddish words that mean, respectively, "to take pride or great joy in someone" and "to complain."

So in 2003, I started the GaGa Sisterhood®[2] to satisfy those needs and to provide a place where grandmas can bond, brag, and benefit.

Our mission is to:

- Inspire each other to stay connected to our grandchildren with as much heart and creativity as possible.
- Provide a forum where we can share our knowledge so that we evolve and become more enlightened grandmas.

We women may have lots of wisdom and years of experience, but we still face new challenges when we become grandmas and feel that we need support and reassurance from other grandmas.

Seven months after becoming a grandma, I decided it was time to tap into that wisdom. I invited all the grandmas I knew to my house to start a conversation about what it means to be a grandma today. On December 7, 2003, fifteen grandmas sat in a circle in my living room—and the GaGa Sisterhood was born.

We told stories about what our grandchildren call us and how we got those names, the great lengths we go to see our grandchildren, how we juggle all our roles to make time for them, and most importantly, how we get along with their sometimes-prickly parents.

There was so much to share and not enough time to dive into everything. We all wanted to continue the conversation. Over the past nine years, more and more grandmas have joined the GaGa Sisterhood and added their wisdom to the mix. We now have a Silicon Valley Chapter, with members from San Rafael to San Jose, and remote members in other parts of the U.S. We've grown into a group of friends with real camaraderie who can laugh about the joys *and* challenges of being a grandma. I realized the role of "grandma" was complicated, and that several grandmas together could figure it out better than one grandma all by herself.

Introduction

One of the biggest misconceptions about becoming a grandma is the belief that it's all about you and your grandchild. I've heard new grandmas rhapsodize over their precious grandchild as if he were a new lover. In fact, they fall so head over heels for that new baby, they lose sight of the bigger picture.

Always keep in mind that the most important component in this grandchild relationship is the child's *parents*. Remember that as you shower your new grandchild with love, attention and gifts. Be sure you show respect and appreciation for his or her parents, too, because when you genuinely appreciate their hard work, they'll trust and respect *you*.

Becoming a grandmother today is a fascinating journey with a steep learning curve. We're learning how to navigate in our new roles right along with our children, the parents of our grandchild. We're all going to make mistakes as we grow into our roles. But if we remember that we're all devoted to the same purpose, nurturing and loving our grandchild, we can overcome problems.

In the nine years since the GaGa Sisterhood began meeting, we've had many enriching conversations on a wide range of topics. But the one that stirs up the most energy and gets everyone talking is, "When Being a Grandma Isn't So Grand."

Sometimes it may seem as if other grandmas don't have any problems. But the reality is, we've all faced challenges of varying degrees at some time. When we share our concerns and listen to what others are going through, we feel comforted knowing we're not alone. Listening to each other's issues with empathy and some humor helps relieve our fears that we're not "doing it right."

Over the years I've heard from GaGa Sisterhood members that sometimes it's too painful for them to attend our meetings because of the conflicts they face in their relationships with the parents of their grandchildren. That's why we've made this topic an annual conversation. The three most common challenges that grandmas identify are:

- Not understanding today's modern parenting methods
- Difficult relationships with their grandchild's parents
- Hurt feelings that result from being unappreciated or left out

Deep down inside us is the unspoken and perhaps irrational fear that if we mess up too badly, we'll lose the privilege of having access to our grandchild. So we tread carefully into the sometimes-choppy waters of this complex relationship with our own children and their spouses and do our best. But because we are all human and have different personalities, we make mistakes.

The most important lesson I've learned since I became a grandma is that if you want access to your grandchild, you must nurture the relationship with his or her parents by building trust and respect. If there are any unresolved issues in your relationships with your children, they're going to surface as you develop a relationship with your grandchild. In order to see your grandchild, you must befriend and respect the gatekeepers!

After listening to grandmas' perspectives for nine years, I thought it was equally important to ask moms how they feel about the grandparent relationship. So I created a survey for moms, with eight questions about the challenges of parenting, their primary sources of conflict, and advice for grandparents. Fifty moms responded; many said that it was a therapeutic experience, to write on the survey what they wished they could say in person to their parents and in-laws.

We have a stake in our grandchildren and want to be part of their lives. Learning where, when, and how much involvement to have is the challenge; it can be made easier if all parties practice open and honest communication, a lofty but often inaccessible goal.

As one mom responded in my survey: *You need to respect me, because if it weren't for me, you wouldn't have grandkids.*

Part I

4 Keys to L.O.V.E. Your Grandchild's Parents

In 1967, John Lennon introduced his award-winning song, *All You Need Is Love*, to the world as a simple message to be understood by all nationalities. But we all know that love is complicated and can be challenging to feel when things are stressful.

Since I've become a grandma, I've learned you need more than love to have a solid relationship with your grandchild's parents. So I've come up with the acronym L.O.V.E. to help remember the four keys to building a loving bond with your grandchild's parents:

Learn the parents' language so that you understand their philosophy.

Own your shared purpose of nurturing a healthy, adjusted child.

Value the parents' hard work and good intentions so that you share mutual respect.

Empathize! Empathize! Empathize! Empathy is infinitely more valuable than advice.

Let's take a closer look at each of these keys.

Chapter One

Learn the Parents' Language

Things have changed since we raised our children. New parents today, who have access to a vast amount of constantly changing information, are open to new ideas about childbirth, delivery, and parenting styles.

There's a whole spectrum of new birth options today. Some expectant mothers want home births, while others want to schedule an induced labor in the hospital so they can plan for the delivery.

Infant gear has become a huge new industry, with ultra-fancy car seats, strollers, co-sleepers, and baby carriers. Playpens are out and play dates are in, even for newborns.

Today's new theories and styles of childrearing may seem very different from the methods we used to raise our children. Learning the parents' style may be one of the *biggest* challenges you will face as a grandma.

Every parent has a parenting style unique to her personality and philosophy on how children should be raised. These styles encompass some basic ideas on discipline, relationship-building, and expectations. Parenting styles can be greatly influenced by what we experienced with our own parents when we were children. Many new parents develop an opposite parenting style to their parents, because their parents' style seemed objectionable or ineffective.

I've heard many new parents describe their own parents' childrearing practices by saying "they did the best they could with what they knew at the time." And, like all new parents, they believe they can do it better. Don't take it personally. Every new generation thinks they've cracked the code on childrearing.

Despite all this wealth of information and self-assuredness, new parents still have lots of insecurities. However, they probably won't admit that to you because they want you to see them as competent and need you to be supportive, observant and complimentary.

In reality, we're all new at these roles. Take the time to sit down with the parents and discuss some of your questions in a non-judgmental way. Begin your education with the mindset of a curious new student. If you want to have access to your new grandchild, you'll need to be open and receptive to your children's parenting "program."

Express genuine interest in what they've been reading and learning. Check out the Internet for a grandparenting class in your community. Many hospitals and medical centers offer seminars to help new grandparents that explain the latest obstetric and pediatric practices so grandparents can get up to speed and understand without having to ask or challenge. Your children will be thrilled that you're taking your new role as a grandparent seriously.

For example, I had never heard of *attachment parenting* or *co-sleeping* before my granddaughter was born. But I soon learned as I watched my daughter carrying her baby in a sling all day long.

The essence of attachment parenting, according to the Attachment Parenting International website[3], is about "forming and nurturing strong connections between parents and their children. The practice of holding the child or keeping it close to the mother's body fulfills a child's need for trust, empathy, and affection and will provide a foundation for a lifetime of healthy relationships. The baby's crying, clinging, and sucking are early techniques to keep her mother nearby. As the child grows and feels more secure in her relationship with her mother, she is better able to explore the world around her and to develop strong, healthy bonds with other important people in her life."

Once I became familiar with the attachment parenting philosophy and witnessed the wonderful results, I was "on board" with their program. I've also become a believer in teaching sign language to babies, making your own baby food, and using new styles of discipline such as the popular "time-outs," also known as "thinking time."

The hallmark of this generation's parents is that they think about parenting a lot. In fact, they have a whole new lexicon when it comes to describing how they parent. In my survey I asked the moms to describe their parenting style. Their responses ranged from the traditional to what some might describe as "wacky" parenting methods[4].

Today's moms tend to be much more conscious or mindful in their parenting than previous generations. Many included the word *presence* when describing their style. Our generation parented *by the seat of our pants*! One mom wrote that she *practices awareness of her own thoughts, emotions, and body before she communicates with her daughter.*

Another explained that her style is constantly evolving due to her children's growth, changing needs, and her own learning. Moms used words like *loving, affectionate,* and *communicative* to describe their parenting style. Parenting choices are often a result of what moms want to model for their children, while consciously practicing presence and simultaneously creating a safe place for them.

Many said they strive to be *authoritative* rather than *authoritarian* by setting clear limits and "giving us both time-outs to pause and listen." Some prefer a "mix of old-school and permissive," while others parent by connection—based on closeness, connection and understanding, along with necessary limits.

Connective parenting[5], a popular new trend, relies on problem-solving and conflict resolution to truly hold a child accountable and responsible. Connective parenting does not rely on the easy methods of parenting—the old standbys. It requires accountability on the mom's part to understand why both she and her child react the way they do and to put in the work necessary to maintain a strong, respectful relationship.

Realistic moms describe themselves as "balanced, authoritative parents, but also have many moments of slipping into indecision, permissiveness or authoritarianism."

Today's moms tend to do research. *Sometimes what I choose to do goes against the previous generation's thoughts...but I'm not worried about it.* Some "old-school" moms believe in "free-range" parenting involving discipline and setting boundaries.

"Free-range" parenting[6] is a commonsense approach to parenting in these overprotective times, coined by Lenore Skenazy, a nationally syndicated columnist and author of *Free-*

Range Kids: Giving Our Children the Freedom We Had Without Going Nuts with Worry. The term "free-range kid" is one who gets treated as a smart, young, capable individual, not someone who needs constant attention and help. At the opposite end of the spectrum are "helicopter moms," who are "risk-averse" and tend to hover over their children.

One mom wrote: *I'm all about creating a child who is independent of me. I believe we borrow our children for a very short time (especially our boys), and we need to give them all our love, support and guidance until they slowly stop taking it. I think some people hold on to their children with two hands and really fear them slipping away. I feel that if you give them the wings to fly, they actually stay connected to you longer.*

One of my favorite responses came from a mom who explained her parenting style as *compassionate, respectful, and fully present. My guiding principle is to treat my children as I would my elderly grandfather—if I wouldn't say something or do something to my grandfather, then I will not say or do it to my children.*

Many moms described themselves as strict but loving, and firm believers in consistency. They have rules that must be followed, especially in terms of safety, and rewards, in terms of privileges.

Today's moms do a lot of explaining to their children, offer them lots of choices, and include them in making decisions. A mom who described herself as firm, loving, and informative, tries to explain things to her children so they understand why she's saying "no" to a particular behavior.

One wise mom advised: *Pick your battles. If he's not going to get hurt and it will still be okay to do the same thing tomorrow, just let it happen. While I'm in charge, not the kids, I try to involve them in a solution when appropriate. I try to be consistent, especially when my son is having a tantrum. I don't give in, and then I process through it with him later.*

Summary

- Adopt the mindset of a curious student.
- Be open and receptive to your children's parenting "program."
- Express genuine interest in what they've been reading and learning.
- Consider taking a grandparenting class in your community.
- New parents research the Internet and make very conscious choices about everything.
- Today's parenting methods cover a wide range of strategies from authoritative to authoritarian and include the children in their decisions.

Journal Activity

What's the biggest difference in today's birth practices compared to when you gave birth to your child?

What observations have you made about your children's parenting style?

What questions would you like to ask them about how they parent?

How does your parenting style compare to your children's?

Chapter Two

Own Your Shared Purpose

Sometimes we grandmas get so caught up in our "love affair" with our grandchild, we forget to spread some of our love and attention on his parents. Many new grandmas are so excited to see their new grandchild, they rush right past the parents, who are standing in the doorway. I've made that blunder with my daughter on more than one occasion.

No matter how much fun it is to play with your grandchildren, it's equally important to make time to connect with their parents. Strengthening that primary relationship and working out the inevitable kinks that come up between parents and adult children, will guarantee a better time with your grandchildren and children.

Another thing we may forget is that we share a common purpose with our grandchild's parents: we all have a stake in the welfare of this child and want him to develop into a healthy, self-actualized human being.

Life is complex for young families. We need to be helpful and take some of the burden off our children so their job is easier. This is how we create goodwill between the generations—when we all have our eye on the same prize and become partners in nurturing our precious grandchildren so they thrive and grow up believing in themselves.

The hard part comes when you *don't* see eye-to-eye with their parents. Then you must help each other understand and respect the other's belief without trying to change them. Strive for diplomacy whenever possible, and take the high road. You'll be a good role model for your children and grandchildren.

Owning your shared purpose is comprised of:

- Committing to the relationship
- Beginning with a closed mouth and an open mind

Commit to Being There

This first step is critical because it sets the tone for a long and loving relationship with your children and grandchild. Getting off to a good start is going to take sensitivity and diplomacy. Listen carefully to what the new parents are saying before the birth and you'll pick up clues about what you can request. What is their birth plan, and will you be included?

I was privileged to witness my granddaughter's birth. My daughter invited me to be present at her delivery. She showed me a copy of her birth plan that explained what she wanted from her doctor and the hospital staff. I respected her requests and my reward was to stand at the foot of her hospital bed and be the first one to see my granddaughter emerge into the world. It was the most miraculous moment of my life and I'll be forever grateful to my daughter and son-in-law for that opportunity.

Not all parents want the grandparents present at the birth, or even just after the birth. Some want to bond alone. Once again, it's important to respect their choice. A young mom I know told her parents she did not want them to visit for three months after her first baby was born. Her mom was crushed. That's not the way she did it when she became a new mom. Her whole family came over to help and offer suggestions.

That was just what my friend feared—too much interference from her mother in this brand new phase of her life. She and her husband are a quiet, reflective couple who are planning a home birth. They want to "hunker down" after the delivery and bond with their newborn without all the intrusion and hovering she fears her mother will bring.

My heart went out to the soon-to-be grandma. I knew she had the best of intentions, but she needs to respect her daughter's wishes and learn to be patient until her daughter feels ready to include her in the "inner circle." This experience will be the first of many for the new grandma when she can't get what she wants. And the more she grasps, the more her daughter will push her away.

Both of these women are anxious about the unknown and the feelings their new roles will bring. The mom has no idea how she's going to feel after giving birth and her mother's pressure to be present is probably intensifying her anxiety. The new grandma is so afraid she's going to miss out and be excluded from her grandchild's life that she's grasping even harder.

The young mom wisely sought the help of a professional to resolve the issue. She and her parents met with a counselor to come up with a solution that worked for all of them. After two weeks of "nesting with their newborn," she and her husband welcomed her parents who stayed at a nearby hotel. Their initial discussion created an understanding that has helped them mutually respect each other's needs.

When you finally do get to meet your new grandchild, you'll want to consider how much time you can devote to visits. Before you talk with your children, think about your responsibilities and how this grandchild will change your life. You actually won't even be able to imagine all the ways your life will be altered. You'll have to juggle your many roles, including this new one, but the payoff is worth the effort.

Maybe you've given some thought to how often you'd like to see your new grandchild. Many factors determine the feasibility and frequency of your visits:

- The physical distance between you and your grandchild
- Your relationship with the parents of your new grandchild
- Your role as the maternal or paternal grandparent
- Your health, energy level and mobility
- Your financial responsibilities and resources
- Everyone's work schedules

Discuss with the new parents what they expect of you and what you expect of them, what help they would like and what help you can give. Be specific about this topic and use your negotiation skills. This is one of the most important conversations you will have. It will show your commitment to the new relationship with your grandchild.

Once you've decided what you're able to commit to, then begin a conversation with the new parents about everyone's wishes and expectations for the frequency and location of visits. This issue will also evolve as the baby gets older and the parents settle into a routine and schedule.

New parents handle the early days following the birth in different ways. Be patient and understanding of their needs to create and nurture their new family unit. This will be your first test of whether you can put aside your own needs and ego. You'll have to accept what arises for you as a new grandma. The more you push for what you want, the more the new parents will resist and push you away.

Other new parents will welcome all the help they can get, and will let you know their plans up front. If you can be there in those first few days after the birth, consider it an honor. You'll be the lucky grandparent who watches in awe as this tiny human being completely enchants and entertains you.

Summary

- Give some love and attention to the parents.
- Strive for diplomacy whenever possible.
- Consider your own needs when negotiating visits.
- Find out the parents' expectations for visitation.
- Be patient, and give the parents time to settle in as a family.

Journal Activity

Describe your ideal visitation plan.
Describe the parents' ideal visitation plan.
What are the expectations regarding childcare?
If you can't be there in person, how can you offer support?

Begin with a closed mouth and an open mind

In June 2011, my daughter and I presented a daylong workshop on "Nurturing the Mother-Daughter Relationship." One of the activities included having the daughters sit in a circle while their mothers sat in a circle around them. The mothers listened in silence while the daughters took turns saying what they wanted in their mother-daughter relationship. Then we switched and asked the mothers to move inside the circle and say what they wanted.

Shared Qualities

Both the mothers and daughters wanted these same qualities in their relationship:

- Acceptance
- Respect
- Communication
- Understanding
- Trust
- Unconditional love
- Non-judgment

Journal Activity

These are the definitions we came up with:

Acceptance: Favorable reception; approval; favor.
What's your definition?

Respect: Esteem for, or a sense of the worth or excellence of, a person.

What's your definition?

Communication: The imparting or interchange of thoughts, opinions, or information.
What's your definition?

Understanding: A state of cooperative or mutually tolerant relations between people.
What's your definition?

Trust: Reliance on the integrity, strength, ability, or surety of a person or thing; confidence.
What's your definition?

Unconditional love: When you love someone the way he or she is, without rules, not the way you want him or her to be. Unconditional love is when you love without expecting anything in return. It is when you love without trying to change someone's behavior and personality.
What's your definition?

Non-judgment: Not condemning another for having a different opinion or way of being that is different from our own. Noticing differences but remaining open to another, rather than closing off to them. Noticing and accepting what is.
What's your definition?

If we can remember to hold these qualities in our hearts when we're interacting with our grandchild's parents, we will reap tremendous rewards from these precious bonds we're building.

But the reality is that it's easier said than done. Our egos and feelings get in the way. We forget that no matter how much wisdom, perspective, and experience we think we've acquired in our long lives, now it's our children's turn to be in charge. They get to "figure it out" while we stand by and witness—sometimes with bated breath and even dismay.

I've found that by practicing these additional qualities, the parents will recognize you as their ally in strengthening the family bond:

- Sensitivity
- Awareness
- Curiosity
- Openness
- Compassion
- Sense of humor

Tips to Improve Mother-Daughter Communication

My daughter and I have learned these tips to improve our communication:

- Make a commitment to understand each other's perspective.
- Agree that you will disagree. It's not about convincing, but understanding the other's point of view.
- Accept each other's choices without judgment.
- Try to resolve a disagreement when it's happening, rather than keeping your feelings inside for days.
- Listen with empathy, not with solutions. Sometimes just saying, "Oh, that must be so hard for you" is all that's needed.
- Use "I" statements, followed by a feeling when you open a discussion.

- Recognize you are both adults and let go of the mother-child dynamic.
- Acknowledge each other when you've expressed your feelings.
- Laugh whenever possible and end with a hug or a "high five."
- Remember the big picture: By modeling good communication, you're setting an example for your grandchildren and the way they speak to you, their siblings and friends.

Summary

- Leave your ego at the door; now it's the parents' turn to make the rules.
- Accept each other's choices without judgment.
- Listen with empathy, not with solutions.

Journal Activity

Can you think of a time when your daughter or daughter-in-law showed signs of feeling left out? What could you do to strengthen the bond between you?

One of the surest ways to win the hearts of your grandchild's parents is to be open to new ideas. Adapt the mindset of a genuinely curious student. Find out what their favorite parenting book is, and read it.

What was the last book your daughter/daughter-in-law read? Find out something she liked about it.

Remember when you were a new parent? What did your parents/in-laws do that bugged you? Consider sharing a story with your grandchild's parents.

Chapter Three

Value The Parents' Hard Work

Respect the Parents' Rules

The most important way to earn your adult children's trust is to respect the rules they've established by following those rules, whether they're present or not. Your reward is that they will feel safe leaving you in charge of your grandchild. They'll know they can call you when they need help and support, and that you'll be there when they call.

One of the best ways to show respect for the parents is to validate their hard work in raising your precious grandchild. There's a difference between validation and patronization, which can get us into trouble. A grandma friend told me she once complimented her son on what a great job he was doing. He responded by saying, "I don't need you to tell me that – I already know I'm doing a good job."

Remember when we were young parents raising our children? All the literature said, catch them doing something right and specifically acknowledge them for it. For example, say, *I love the way you comfort the baby when she's crying.*

New parents can be especially touchy when it comes to grandma's comments. Even the most benign statement can trigger a defensive reaction. One grandma told me she offered to wash the dishes and her daughter-in-law got defensive. She interpreted her request as a judgment on her ability to do a good job herself.

One of the fascinating aspects of becoming a grandparent is the new relationship you'll have with your grandchild's parents. Your roles will now be reversed. That child you raised will now be the one making the rules, and you'll be expected to follow them. Or at least try very hard to follow them, if you want time alone with your grandchild.

We have to understand and respect our children's child-rearing practices if we want to build a close relationship with both generations. I once let my three-year-old granddaughter have a cookie, and the first thing she did when we got home was to run and tell her mommy! She was so excited she couldn't contain herself My daughter forgave me, but I didn't make that mistake again. What you do is going to get back to the parents and you're going to lose your credibility.

Learning to respect your adult children involves understanding each other, listening to their language, and respecting their boundaries.

By simply observing what's going on with an open mind, you will begin to understand the rules and structures the parents are trying to implement. This may be the hardest part of the process, because their methods may seem foreign to you. You may not agree with their philosophy, but remember it's *their* learning process and our role is to be supportive, empathic cheerleaders.

Remember to stay in a place of non-judgment and whatever you may be thinking, *don't roll your eyes!* As grandmothers, we think our expressions are neutral. In reality, our feelings are visible and readily obvious to our children and grandchildren. We're often unaware that a raised eyebrow, a shrug of a shoulder, a deep sigh, or looking the other way can show displeasure.

Like most people, when parents feel judged, they get defensive and upset. They need your support and encouragement to believe that they're succeeding as parents. Remember, no matter how confident they may appear, deep down inside they're feeling insecure about whether they're doing it the "right way"—especially since there are so many new parenting strategies floating around today.

One of the best ways to understand your adult children is to sit down with them and have a conversation about why they believe in the theories they're implementing. Try to see the issue from their point of view. Listen to the language that your children are using to parent. There's a whole new lexicon in the world of parenting, and it's worth doing some research so you'll have a greater appreciation of this new breed of parents.

If you're lucky enough to have your grandchild stay over, ask if the rules can be relaxed at your house during those visits. It's also important to establish your own house rules for the occasions when your grandchild visits.

You will make mistakes as you adjust to the new parents' rules. *Everyone* is learning their new roles, and nobody knows how they should behave. Our role, thankfully, is to be the *entertainers*, not the *enforcers*. We did our stint as the disciplinarians when we raised our children, so now we get to sit back and enjoy.

Warning: You may get complaints or feelings of envy from the parents when you're having so much fun that you're behaving like a child yourself. My daughter has told me on more than one occasion that she doesn't like being the enforcer while I get to have all the fun. But that's another benefit of being a grandparent versus being a parent. We're not responsible for raising our grandchildren. Respecting your children's rules will guarantee you more face time with your grandchild and will earn your trust from his or her parents.

Summary

- Respect the parents' rules.
- Be specific when you validate a parent.
- Learn their parenting vocabulary.
- Expect to make mistakes, and be quick to apologize.

Journal Activity

Write down one new parenting idea your children have embraced.
What was the last behavior you observed in the parents that you disagreed with?
How did you handle it?
What was their reaction?
How could you have done it differently?

Chapter Four

Empathize! Empathize! Empathize!

Empathy is the capability to share and understand another's emotions and feelings. It is often characterized as the ability to "put oneself into another's shoes."

One of the most important things I've learned as a grandma is that empathy has more value than advice or problem-solving. It's natural to offer suggestions when we hear our children complaining. But they don't want solutions; they want us to hear what they're saying and feel what they're experiencing.

Several years ago, my daughter complained to me about the mean girls in my granddaughter's class. Without giving it much thought, I replied: "Oh, that's what kids do in the first grade!"

Boy, did I blow it with my off-handed remark—on two counts! First of all, if I'd listened more carefully, I would have remembered to empathize, which my daughter is always reminding me to do. Second, I completely minimized her distress.

A few days later, we talked about our conversation and she admitted that my response bothered her. I said I needed to create a bumper sticker with these words: EMPATHIZE, DON'T MINIMIZE.

She loved the idea. All she wanted me to say was, "It must be so hard to watch that mean behavior," affirm what she was feeling, and then commiserate a little. For example, "I remember when you were little and the kids teased you. I felt so helpless, I didn't know what to do."

Empathize, Don't Minimize has become my mantra because that's what the parents of our grandchildren want. And for that matter, all the people in our lives want empathy[7]. Being a problem-solver, I have to constantly remind myself that people don't want advice; they want you to understand how they're feeling.

Another way to focus on empathy is to think before you speak, by taking a long, slow, deliberate breath. I've been guilty of speaking without thinking and it's gotten me into trouble more times than I care to admit.

There are two schools of thought on whether to speak up or bite your tongue. Ruth Nemzoff suggests the former in her book: *Don't Bite Your Tongue: How to Foster Rewarding Relationships with Your Adult Children*. (Palgrave Macmillan, New York, NY 2008)

In her chapter on grandparenting, she observes that because of increased life expectancy, today's grandparents can expect to live long enough to see their grandchildren married, and may even get to enjoy great-grandchildren. In that case, we will witness our children and grandchildren go through many different stages that will require us to find new ways of interacting with them.

"When your children make it clear they don't want your input on a given topic," writes Nemzoff, "then respect that, and save your breath for an area where your input *is* sought. Your children will be more likely to listen to *you*, if they feel you're listening to *them*. Timing is everything."

Those ways of interacting require a great deal of sensitivity and restraint. Other grandmas have said they share my concerns when it comes to "weighing my words carefully." I joke to my friends that when I visit my granddaughters, I roll out the eggshell carpet and tread very carefully, lest my words or actions be misinterpreted by their parents.

A grandma friend got into trouble for commenting several times that her son and daughter-in-law were treating their little boy like a royal. "They really do fawn over him," she told me.

Today's parents include their children in all their plans and often ask their children's preferences in making decisions. This practice can seem overindulgent to grandparents and even more so to great-grandparents, who still may believe that children should be seen and not heard. I've witnessed my mother roll her eyes when we've been at a restaurant and her great-grandchild gets to decide where everyone sits at the table.

Even when we try to "zip it," our body language often shows our true feelings, to which we are entitled. Body language can be used to communicate positive unspoken feelings as well as negative ones. A huge smile, a hug, a slight nod or a touch or squeeze of a hand speak volumes.

I try to be very conscious and respectful when I talk to my daughter and son-in-law. Our intention is to understand each other because we share a common purpose: to provide a life for these two girls that will help them thrive and use their gifts in the world.

Summary

- Empathy has more value than advice or problem-solving.
- Take a breath and think for a moment before you speak.
- Be aware of your body language, which could be sending a negative message.

Journal Activity
What are your dreams for your grandchild?
What are the parents' dreams for their child?
What is your shared purpose?

A Few Final Words of Reassurance

Ruth Nemzoff recommends "the way to enjoy grandparenting is to relax, to stop judging, and to realize that there are many ways to bring up healthy, considerate people."

So how do we follow her advice? As the late Richard Carlson advised in his 1997 book, *Don't Sweat the Small Stuff* – instead, focus on the good stuff. Step back and look at the big picture. If your grandchild is thriving, then it doesn't matter what you think. You may not agree with your children's parenting methods, but that doesn't mean one is right and one is wrong.

Each generation has a new approach to parenting — they want to see if they can do it better than we did. It's one more part of finding their own identities. Trust your children that they've done their research and now want to test their own judgment, not yours. The only reason to intervene would be if you see abuse or neglect. Otherwise, we need to stand on the sidelines and be a cheerleader for the parents.

It's so hard, because we're still in the parent mode and we just want to help our children. But they must learn for themselves. Try asking your children what *they* think would be a good solution, versus volunteering too much advice. We need to empower the new parents, help them believe they're the best parents for their child, and make them feel comfortable and confident in their new roles.

Otherwise, "our children hear the deeper messages—the meaning behind our words, our anxieties, our disapproval," says Nemzoff. She suggests you ask yourself these questions:

Do the things that bother me about the way my children raise their children really matter?

Are my grandchildren in danger?

If we think their actions make life more difficult for our children, but they are willing to pay the price in lost sleep or tantrums, why should we care?

One grandma told me she keeps three words in her head whenever she's around her granddaughter's mom: *supportive*, *observant* and *complimentary*. She says it's helped her be able to hear things from a new mom's viewpoint. She's become more sensitive to her daughter-in-law and as a grandparent, she's created a new relationship with her.

This new relationship with our grandchild's parents can be one of the biggest surprises in becoming a grandparent. We expect it's going to be all about bonding with our new grandchild when in fact, we're spending much more time with that child's parents. The good news is that if you didn't get it right when you raised that child of yours, you now have a second chance.

You can take advantage of the opportunity to renew the bond with your grandchild's parents by remembering to schedule time with them. Whenever I visit my grandchildren, I make sure to plan an activity with my daughter. We take walks or go out for coffee so that we have time for just the two of us. Without that private time, our relationship can get overshadowed by all the attention we shower on our grandchildren. Parents can get envious and feel left out. They need our love and nurturing, too. The more you bond with your children, the more comfortable they'll feel about letting you bond with your grandchildren.

One mom responded to my survey by saying: *I would not allow my mother access to my children if she were not in a sound relationship with me. At first she thought it didn't matter how well she was connecting with me, that she could just come and relate directly to my children. But as a new mother (think "mama bear"), this did not sit right with me at all. I made it clear that she needed to be in a reasonably comfortable relationship with me in order for me to be willing for her to relate to my children.*

Now that we have more life experience under our belt, we can appreciate how difficult it is to parent. We can have more empathy and perspective on what truly matters. As parents, it's often easier to swallow our pride when conflict arises and practice graciously saying, "I'm sorry, I've made a mistake." Trust me, it gets easier with repetition.

In my own experience, I've learned that parents get more flexible as they gain more confidence and experience. My daughter has relaxed the rules significantly with her second child compared to her first-born.

Summary

- Trust your children's decisions that they've done their research on parenting.
- Don't volunteer advice. Ask them what *they* think would be a good solution.
- Be supportive, observant, and complimentary.
- Schedule time to spend with your grandchild's parents.

Journal Activity

What parenting practice do you have questions about?
What is it that bothers you about this practice?
What can you do to help yourself feel better about this practice?

Part II

The Mom's Perspective

And Now a Word From the Moms

Sage Advice:
There are many "right" ways to do things.
Honesty. I wish they would just be honest with me. No excuses, just simple honesty. No beating around the bush, just say what you think.
Positive words, or bite your tongue.

Moms' Survey Results

For the past nine years I've been listening to the grandma's perspective in the grandparent relationship. I realized that in order to help us grandmothers improve our relationship with our grandchild's parents—especially their mothers—we need to hear what moms have to say about *their* role in the grandparent relationship.

I conducted my own survey to find out directly from moms what their biggest challenges are. After reading over 50 responses, I felt even more compassion for today's moms and their ability to withstand all the pressures they face.

Since becoming a grandma, I've developed tremendous empathy for today's moms. There is broad agreement among the public that it is harder to be a parent today than when we were raising *our* children. And I completely agree.

A national survey by the Pew Research Center[8], conducted in 2007 among 2,000 Americans, found a widespread belief that today's parents are not measuring up to the standard that parents set a generation ago. Can you imagine how parents must feel under this degree of stigma?

The biggest challenge in raising children today, according to parents and non-parents alike, is dealing with the outside influences of society. Among the top specific concerns mentioned in the survey are drugs and alcohol, peer pressure, and the impact of television and other media.

Beyond societal influences, other challenges in raising children include teaching morals and values, maintaining discipline, handling the financial aspects of childrearing, and dealing with the educational system.

I invite you to take a moment and imagine you're a mom raising young children today. One of the biggest challenges you'll face is the vast amount of new and conflicting information about parenting available on the Internet, which is where today's moms spend a lot of time.

Here are some of the moms' responses about the challenges they face:

- *Raising my kids in a culture that seems hell-bent on tearing down families is my biggest challenge.*

- *There is so much going on in society nowadays that feels like it's working against what I believe is best for my children. It can be exhausting.*
- *I feel like I'm up against a world that has its morals backwards. One of my goals as a mother has been to raise good kids with good morals. When morals are valued least in our society, it's a tough row to hoe.*
- *It's impossible to keep the negative media messages away from my children.*

Mompetition

Moms face an even more insidious challenge when other mothers' harsh judgment of them gets internalized. There's an overwhelming amount of external pressure on today's moms, which makes them more competitive with each other than our generation was. It starts the minute they have their first child and are asked:

- *Was the birth a natural delivery or C-section?*
- *Are you breastfeeding or giving a bottle?*
- *Do you use cloth or disposable diapers?*
- *Do you make your own baby food or buy it at the grocery store?*

I learned about "mompetition" from a post titled When Moms Verbally Attack Each Other, We All Lose[9] by Christina Simon of *Beyond the Brochure.* Simon quotes child and adolescent psychotherapist Katie Hurley, who writes the popular blog, Practical Parenting[10]. Hurley believes that "competition often stems from an internal struggle with what she refers to as 'Mom-Esteem[11]' or how moms feel about their choices as moms and their ability to effectively parent their children."

"The fact is that all families, and all children, are different," says Hurley. "But moms today seem to think there is one 'right' way to parent. In an effort to feel better about the parenting style they've chosen, some moms will lash out at or criticize other moms. At its very core, it really boils down to bullying. They want to feel right and powerful, so they hurt others along the way. Unfortunately, no one wins when moms go on the attack. If the children hear the exchanges, they stand a lot to lose, as this is not a healthy way to treat other people…regardless of whether or not you agree with the choices being made."

Two moms from my survey wrote about their "Mom-Esteem" issues:

- *I have the mommy complex of needing to be the one who volunteers for everything so the other moms will approve. I put too much pressure on myself.*
- *I don't know if I'm measuring up because I have no idea what expectations and goals I should meet.*

Moms worry constantly whether they're making the right decisions for their children. And it's no wonder. With so many conflicting choices, it can be overwhelming trying to figure out the right thing to do. When we were moms, we didn't question some of these basic decisions: whether to vaccinate our children, whether to send them to school or home school, whether to feed them organic food. Today's moms worry about vaccinations, the negative influences in schools and the media, and our food supply, just to name a few concerns.

Moms of every generation can empathize with the dreaded "daily grind" we face as moms. One described motherhood as "mundane and thankless." Others complained about feeling exhausted and impatient, and constantly being interrupted. *I can't complete a thought without someone asking me for something.*

Moms feel like they never get any time for themselves or their husbands. And even their children get short shrift, as one mom complained: *It's hard to remember to take time to enjoy my children when housework or just work gets in the way.*

The constancy of the demands on their energy, time, brain, and body can be completely draining, especially when they're worrying about whether they're disciplining the right way and staying consistent.

One respondent observed a significant difference between today's moms and our generation of moms. Most of us grandmas were younger when we gave birth to our children. The impact on the mother's age can mean two things: younger moms have more energy, and can space their children's births farther apart.

According to a study by familyfacts.org, since 1970, the average age of mothers giving birth to their first child has increased from 21 to 25 years. Many women are postponing motherhood until the age of 25 to 29 years old. Also, there's a significant increase in first-time mothers between the ages of 35 and 40, due to advances in obstetrics and fertility and lower risks in pregnancies.

Another significant difference in today's generation of mothers is their need to work outside the home. A recent report from the Bureau of Labor Statistics on employment characteristics of families stated that 70% of moms with children under 18 are in the work force. The employment rate for mothers with children under 6 years old is only slightly lower, at 64%.

Moms who work outside the home described these challenges:

- *I'm not able to enjoy my kids at night when I'm also trying to catch up on the domestic responsibilities that await me when I get home.*
- *I try not to disappoint my child when I feel like I should be all things to everyone.*
- *Everything is on me whether I'm working full time or staying home because I'm just naturally the director of the ship.*
- *I never have enough time, and then I worry it will all be over too soon.*
- *It's so hard to get ready on school mornings when no one wants to get up, move, or cooperate.*
- *When siblings are just picking on each other all day, I wish I could call in sick on parenthood, like I can at work!*
- *I hate struggling with the chaos in my house all the time and feeling like I'm always nagging them.*

More than one mom lamented that the constancy of parenting can be so draining, they fantasize about how to deal with it.

- *Sometimes I just want to go home to a studio apartment with all-white furniture and read in complete silence.*
- *On a good day I think I make some strong parenting choices, and on a bad day I say to myself, like in the commercial, "Calgon, take me away."*

Conflicts and Misunderstandings

Misunderstandings, hurt feelings, and breakdowns in communication are the terrain of grandmotherhood. The best way to resolve them is to be able to honestly share how you are feeling and what's making you feel that way, whether you're a mom or a grandma. But as one mom wrote: *Speaking up is not always comfortable for me and doesn't come easily.*

Some grandparents are more open to a dialog than others. Some have dealt with their baggage, and others have not. It can be even more difficult for a grandma, especially a mother-in-law, to speak her mind, for fear of alienating her daughter-in-law.

In my survey, I asked moms to describe the most common areas of conflict with grandparents. Overindulgence in any area irritates parents, whether it's too much sugar and junk food, too much television, or inappropriate gifts and toys.

Equally frustrating are grandparents who don't follow the parents' rules and question their parental decisions, such as insisting on a pacifier or solid food when a baby cries.

Moms also complained about grandparents physically disciplining their grandchildren, judging a grandchild's behavior, or badmouthing a mom in front of her kids.

Moms want grandmas to be more direct when they communicate and not display such passive-aggressive behaviors as eye-rolling or shoulder-shrugging. Moms don't appreciate us offering our constant opinions or telling them how to parent—it's a "turn-off."

Mom's Wish List

In my survey I asked moms what they wished they could say to the grandparents. Most of their poignant responses fell into two categories: they want RESPECT and EMPATHY. Below are the moms' own words:

Respect

Moms don't appreciate grandmas who believe that the best thing about grandparenting is that we can spoil the kids and then send them home. Kids will respect us more if we have some rules, just like home. Then, when the parents get the kids back, they don't have to "re-teach" manners and rules.

Remember that times change, circumstances change and you cannot expect your grandchildren to be raised the same way that you raised your children. And by the way, if you believe you raised your children well, you should have faith in the way they raise their children.

My way of parenting is just different, and works for me, as they felt their way worked for them.

Sometimes I am so caught up in correcting my parents or proving something, that I forget to just thank them for doing the best they could and letting them know how much I love them.

Respect our rules and don't question our decisions in front of the grandchildren. Don't tell us how to parent.

I wish the grandparents understood and accepted that, YES, some of the parenting choices we make are a result of things that didn't work for us in our childhood. But it doesn't mean we love them any less and it doesn't mean we are trying to make them wrong. Some of the choices are simply based on the new information that comes out all the time. We have the opportunity to improve our practices with each generation.

I wish the grandparents would get how much it hurts when they ignore, resist, or disrespect our choices.

I always have my child's best interests in mind, and I think they know this. But they just disagree on what that looks like. I think that when my children have grown and all the grandparents can see that they did, in fact, turn out to be happy, respectful, healthy, generous, mature, successful adults, then they will feel comfortable knowing that it worked.

My choices may look different than hers, but it's because I have different information coming to me. I respect her choices, knowing they were the best she could make at that time, but now I see something different and am able to make different choices.

Thank you for being part of our lives. We love you and you are important to us. Please don't personalize times when we aren't as doting and attentive as you want. We're just maxed out sometimes with work, school, and activities. But it doesn't mean you don't matter to us. You do!

Don't try and be disciplinarians, rather just be their friends. Leave the parenting to the parents.

I wish they would appreciate that we try to feed our kids healthily. I don't mind the kids having treats at their house, but when they know we don't like them to have soda and treats before dinner and give it to them anyway, it's not only annoying, it's hurtful. I want them to be proud of us for the healthy habits we're trying to instill in the kids, not roll their eyes at us.

Empathy

Moms want us to be patient—with ourselves and with them. They wish we would remember what it was like to raise our kids and how we felt about all the "advice" everyone was willing to offer us. By following that wish, they hope we'll give more unconditional love and support and listen more so that we understand them.

I wish my parents would understand that our generation (for better or worse) is perhaps more self-centered than their generation.

I wish my parents "got" how deeply I would love to share what's going on without having them take it on as their "project" – to care without advice or solutions. (This request can be difficult for those of us who are "problem-solvers." So go back and re-read the section *Empathy Empathy Empathy* to remind yourself that moms want to be *heard,* not *advised*!)

Have a presence in your grandchildren's lives at the different stages as they grow. The more time you spend with them, the more you can understand them. Support the parents by helping out in different areas.

My parents get upset when we don't answer the phone. They have no idea what may be happening at that time. Sometimes we're in the middle of a frenzy with the kids and other times we're all enjoying our time together as a family (or just the two of us) and we don't want to lose the momentum by answering the phone and having to pretend everything is great.

My parents never want to hear about anything being wrong. Just once I'd like them to ask: "How is everything with YOU? I know parenting is hard, on top of trying to nurture a marriage and work outside of the house so that you can get out of financial debt. We enjoy having the kids and hope it's helpful to you. Is there anything we can do to help you and your spouse in other ways? Marriage is important, so would you like to schedule a few date nights and we'll take the kids so you can have time alone together?"

I'd like us to enjoy each other's company more. I'd like my dad to be able to listen and acknowledge how hard I work. I'd like him to tell me he's proud of me for my accomplishments.

When you call your kids, ask if it's a good time to talk, and assure them that if it's not, you can talk later. When we don't answer the phone, don't leave angry messages about why we aren't answering. That doesn't make us want to call you back. Just say, "Hi, I'd love to talk to you and see how you are. Please call me when it's convenient."

Check in with your kids about how THEY are doing with all that's on their plates, not just how your grandchildren are doing.

Sometimes I feel as if my mom is missing out on her grandchildren's lives. We live about two hours apart and although she is very responsive and willing to "help," she is not very available to visit for unscheduled down time with the kids. I feel this is so important for developing a close relationship. Sometimes I feel like my mom is very engrossed in the minutiae of her own life and missing the big picture of her grandmother role. She expects us to come to her, which we often do, but at some point I wish she could join in the rhythm of our life.

I would prefer to have a relationship where I could share more openly about my perspective and give my mother-in-law some insight into why I do the things I do. However, in the past when conversations have gone in this direction, I've felt judged instead of understood. Therefore it feels safer to keep the relationship as it is. But as a result, I don't think she is as connected to us as a family.

Advice to grandparents

Many moms who responded to my survey said it was cathartic to answer the questions, especially the one asking what they wish they could say to the grandparents. They'd like us to read articles that support their choices and talk about them together so that we have a better understanding of their parental decisions.

Moms believe we can improve our relationship with them and the grandchildren by being part of their lives as "everyday" grandparents. If we can offer acts of service, such as carpooling, babysitting, paying for the grandchild's activities, these are most helpful. If we can be available to visit for unscheduled down time with the grandchildren, that will help develop a close relationship

Here are some of the mom's suggestions:

You had your chance to raise a child. Now your job is to give tons and tons of unconditional love. If you were asked for your opinion on the baby's name or where the kid should go to school, that's great. If you were not asked, perhaps your opinion wasn't required. Know when to take a step back.

Honesty. I wish they would just be honest with me. No excuses, just simple honesty. No beating around the bush, just say what you think.

Both my parents and my husband's parents are now gone, but I hope they are somehow aware of what amazing individuals share some of their genes.

I wish the grandparents would make more effort. We parents are harried and busy and time slips by. We don't mean to ignore the grandparents, but we're just too preoccupied with "putting out fires." The grandparents should roll out the invitations and make time with the grandkids. Own their experience and understand that our generation is pulled in several directions. We seem to have an entire generation suffering from attention deficit and flakiness. Any help from our elders would benefit both the grandkids and the grandparents.

Have a regular time to talk every week and talk to each parent separately.

Find things to enjoy together between parent and grandparent without the grandchild.

Assume good intentions. Your daughter-in-law is not out to hurt your feelings.

Have a presence in your grandchildren's life at the different stages as they grow. The more time you spend with them, the more you'll understand them.

COMMUNICATE: that's what makes all the difference. If I don't like how my folks are handling a situation, we talk about it.

Check in with your kids about how THEY are doing with all that's on their plates, not just how your grandchildren are doing. When your kids do need you to step aside and not get involved, step aside graciously but let them know you're there when they need you.

The parent knows the child better than you. Let them be the parent. Trust them. Help them when they ask for it.

Grandparent with the parents' philosophies in mind. If you have questions about their parenting method, ask questions or do *your own research. Provide empathy and support to the parents. If you have resources, ask how you can help with money and time to be supportive. Know that parenting is VERY different than when you were a parent, and things are very different for your grandchildren than they were for your children. **Don't minimize parents' concerns**.*

Try to see things through their eyes. Your children have a different situation than your household, and they will do some things differently. That can be OK, too. Also, they have to make mistakes as parents, just like you did.

Don't put my children on a pedestal. Ask the parents what they feel are appropriate toys to give as gifts.

Be active and be present. Don't just sit there doing your own thing. Try to really engage with what the child is doing. This is your time to enjoy, to be a child again, so take that opportunity, and leave the hard work and discipline to the parents.

Relationships need work constantly. My folks feel that their kids are grown and now their work is done. For me, that's hurtful. Their apathy is much harder to take than any meddling ever could.

Grandparents are uniquely able to love and support grandkids and their parents if they do not feel that they need to be in control of parenting decisions.

Journal Activity

Which of these quotes from moms resonates with you, and why?

Conclusion

A grandma friend once asked me: Do you think as grandmas we keep our lips zipped because deep down inside us there's an irrational fear that our grandchildren might someday be withheld from us?

Victoria Zackheim addresses this issue in her powerful essay "A Balancing Act of Love," from *The ART of Grandparenting*. After she became conscious of this fear, she asked her grandma friends and was surprised to discover that nearly every one of them carried that same fear.

I know grandmas who've been told by their own children that any visits with their grandchildren must be supervised. But I don't personally know any who've been banned from seeing their grandchildren.

Zackheim reminds us that the relationship between grandchildren and grandparents is totally parent-dependent until the grandchildren grow up and can make their own choices. So it *is* important to ensure that you create as few ripples as possible.

Sadly, grandparent alienation does exist and affects many families across the country. Susan Hoffman, founder of Advocates for Grandparent Grandchild Connection[12], knows first-hand the pain of being estranged from a grandchild. She wrote about it in her first book, *Grand Wishes* published in

2008. She sponsored a grandparents' rights bill that became law in 2007.

Hoffman has written a second book, *A Precious Bond*, which focuses on what she's learned since then. She offers grandparents advice on how to avoid the behaviors that lead to estrangement. She emphasizes the importance of recognizing that you can't change someone else's behavior. If you want to see a different outcome, you have to change your own behavior.

The book includes a list of DO's and DON'Ts to help grandparents avoid some of the common mistakes that can lead to break downs in communication between families. I decided to include her list, not to strike unnecessary fear in your heart but because her advice is valuable for ALL grandparents in building mutual respect and avoiding power struggles between you and your adult children.

DO:
Forgive
Listen
Respect parent's boundaries
Pay attention to parents
Include parents in conversation
Include parents in activities
Consult with parent before giving gifts
Ask permission before visiting
Check before taking the child places
Go with the flow
Follow parent's rules
Apologize

DON'T:
Lose temper
Defend actions

Argue
Give advice
Ignore parent's boundaries
Discount parent's rules
Criticize or complain
Have expectations of how things should be
Take everything personal
Manipulate to suit own desires
Ask "why"
Exclude the parent
Ask the child to keep secrets
Triangulate
Make ultimatums or appear threatening

The Last Word

I'll let the moms have the last word here. A mom in my survey said she loves her mother-in-law because she always follows the 3 Cs Rule:

- *No comments*
- *No criticism*
- *No complaints*

As grandmothers, we'd be wise to remember these three simple rules. In doing so, we'll preserve peace in the family and earn our children's respect and appreciation.

Bibliography

Connelly, Valerie. *The Art of Grandparenting: Loving, spoiling, teaching, and playing with your grandkids.* Mequon, WI: Nightengale Press, 2009. (Includes my chapter: "How to Become a Go-to Grandma.")

Carson, Lillian. *The Essential Grandparent: A guide to making a difference.* Deerfield Beach, FL: Health Communications, 1996.

Fisher, Ellie Slott. *It's Either Her or Me: A Guide to Help a Mom and Her Daughter-in-Law Get Along.* New York, NY. Random House, 2010.

Graham, Barbara. *Eye of My Heart: 27 Writers reveal the hidden pleasures and perils of being a grandmother.* New York, NY: Harper Collins, 2009.

Hoffman, Susan. *A Precious Bond: How to preserve the grandparent-grandchild relationship.* New Delhi, India: Collegare Press, 2011.

Hough, Lindy. *Wondrous Child: The Joys and Challenges of Grandparenting.* Berkeley, CA: North Atlantic Books, 2012.

Isay, Jane. *Walking on Eggshells: Navigating the Delicate Relationship Between Adult Children and Parents.* New York, NY: Random House, 2007.

Johnson, Sue and Carlson, Julie. *Grandloving: Making memories with your grandchildren.* Lancaster, VA: Heartstrings Press, 2010.

Kornhaber, Arthur. *The Grandparent Guide: The definitive guide to coping with the challenges of modern grandparenting.* New York, NY: McGraw-Hill, 2002.

Lara, Adair. *The Granny Diaries: An insider's guide for new grandmothers.* San Francisco, CA: Chronicle Books, 2008.

Nemzoff, Ruth. *Don't Bite Your Tongue: How to Foster Rewarding Relationships with Your Adult Children.* New York, NY: Palgrave Macmillan, 2008.

Olds, Sally Wendkos. *Super Granny: Great stuff to do with your grandkids.* New York, NY: Sterling Publishing Co., 2009.

Skenazy, Lenore. *Free-Range Kids: How to Raise Safe, Self-Reliant Children (Without Going Nuts with Worry).* San Francisco, CA: Jossey-Bass, 2010.

Sophy, Charles. *Side By Side: The Revolutionary Mother-Daughter Program for Conflict-free Communication.* New York, NY: Harper Collins, 2010

Endnotes

[1] http://bit.ly/SHRmlh Vacation Journals Save Precious Memories
[2] http://gagasisterhood.com/ GaGa Sisterhood
[3] http://www.attachmentparenting.org/ Attachment Parenting International
[4] http://bit.ly/yYT7Ft Five Wacky Parenting Methods
[5] http://bit.ly/MwQuAM Connective Parenting philosophy
[6] http://freerangekids.wordpress.com/ Free-Range Kids
[7] http://teachempathy.com/ Learn more about empathy and how empathy can enrich your life.
[8] http://bit.ly/Ob5ikE Pew Research Study on Motherhood Today
[9] http://bit.ly/yZ0uhk When Moms Verbally Attack Each Other, We All Lose on Mamapedia Voices
[10] http://practicalkatie.com/ Practical Parenting
[11] http://bit.ly/grioXs Mom Esteem: How Do You Rate Yours?
[12] http://bit.ly/MlyiZ0 Advocates for Grandparent Grandchild Connection

About the Author

Donne Davis is passionate about connecting with other grandmas to explore what it means to be a grandma today. After she became a grandma in 2003, she founded the GaGa Sisterhood (gagasisterhood.com), a social network for enthusiastic grandmas. Her mission is to inspire grandmas to find creative ways to stay connected with their grandchildren *and* their parents.

She has contributed to two grandparent anthologies: *The ART of Grandparenting* and *Wondrous Child: The Joys and Challenges of Grandparenting*. She writes a monthly column called "The Go-to Grandma" for Parenting on the Peninsula, as well as her GaGa Sisterhood blog, which features resources, activities, and inspiration for grandmas and their families. She also speaks on a variety of grandparenting topics.

Her two granddaughters are her favorite playmates. Their lively imaginations constantly reignite the child in her. She lives in the San Francisco Bay Area.